Mitra Tabrizian

Mitra Tabrizian

This is That Place

T.J. Demos and Rose Issa

Tate Publishing

First published 2008
by order of the Tate Trustees
by Tate Publishing, a division
of Tate Enterprises Ltd,
Millbank, London SW1P 4RG
www.tate.org.uk/publishing

on the occasion of the exhibition
Mitra Tabrizian: This is That Place

Tate Britain, London
3 June – 10 August 2008

British Library Cataloguing in
Publication Data
A catalogue record for this book
is available from the British Library

ISBN 978-1-85437-814-9

Designed by Fraser Muggeridge studio
Printed by BAS, Hampshire

Front cover: Mitra Tabrizian,
Tehran 2006, 2006 (detail)

Measurements of artworks are given
in centimetres, height before width

Foreword

Mitra Tabrizian was born in Tehran, Iran and has lived in London since 1977. Her carefully constructed photographs offer a challenging critique of corporate culture and contemporary life, touching a range of issues and debates: from post-feminism and post-colonial theories and the effects of late capitalism in Britain, to the shifting realities of life in post-revolutionary Iran.

Tate Britain is delighted to present Tabrizian's first solo exhibition at a major museum in Britain. It brings together a selection of works from 2001 to 2007 which explore, in particular, themes of social fragmentation, the homeland and the reality of exile. Collectively, they highlight Tabrizian's approach to constructed picture-making, drawing on filmic conventions to create concise and potent narratives.

Many individuals have helped bring this project to fruition. Above all I thank Rose Issa, the exhibition's curator, for her clear vision and commitment throughout. I would also like to thank T.J. Demos for his thoughtful essay and Fraser Muggeridge and Sarah Newitt for their elegant design. In addition I would like to thank Jananne Al-Ani, Sarah Derry, Camilla Edwards, Rana Kabbani, Kristine Von Oehsen, Andrea Rose and Gilane Tawadros. At Tate Britain Clarrie Wallis has led the project from the start, with important contributions from Felicity Allen, Jennifer Batchelor, Helen Beeckmans, Sarah Briggs, Louise Butler, Sionaigh Durrant, Claire Eva, Will Gompertz, Sofia Karamani, Brad MacDonald, Judith Nesbitt, Mary Richards, Andy Shiel, Roger Thorp and Emma Woodiwiss.

Finally, our special thanks go to Mitra Tabrizian herself for giving time, energy and insight so generously to this project.

Stephen Deuchar
Director, Tate Britain

Beyond the Limits … of Photography
T.J. Demos

In Mitra Tabrizian's *Border*, a suite of photographs from 2005–6, isolated figures appear lost in thought, caught in moments of reverie stolen from everyday life. Parvaneh leans against a wall near a stairwell, pausing before a sign that reads 'circle', suggesting the repetitive cycles of workaday existence. And Rasool, a young man pictured holding a bouquet of flowers, rests on his parked scooter on a pathway near a forest, gazing into the distance, seemingly questioning the commitment he is about to make. Time has momentarily stopped for these people, their far-off thoughts leaving their inert bodies behind. As we learn from Tabrizian's descriptions, all of them have crossed borders, coming to the UK from Iran to find a better life. Yet it is clear in these photographs that they have also brought those borders with them, remaining painfully divided between their present circumstances and the longings for home, or their aching to feel at home, elsewhere.

While Tabrizian's earlier work, including *Beyond the Limits* (2000–1) and *Lost Time* (2002), has frequently focused on the social dislocation of figures situated in generic environments such as corporate interiors and suburban parks, *Border* marks a shift in her oeuvre. Its portraiture of real individuals distinguishes it from her longstanding exploration of photography's post-documentary status following the era of postmodern simulation. Nevertheless, while *Border* alters Tabrizian's thematic focus from non-specific corporate types to actual immigrants, the series continues her investigation of the way in which social displacement is expressed through photography. The power of the medium to disconnect image from referent results in scenes of uncertainty that rupture the continuity of quotidian life.

This photographic uncertainty can be explained by both the technological advances of photographic imaging and the wider cultural conditions in which those advances are set. Certainly a key factor has been the development of digital imagery and post-production procedures since the 1980s, which have meant that photography can artificially construct just about any scene imaginable, such as a man falling from a tall building, or a letter ripped up and flung to the wind, or a woman positioned perilously in the middle of a motorway – all of which make their appearance in various pieces by Tabrizian. The digital image does not offer an indexical sign – like a footprint or a shadow – of something real, which typifies analogue photography (what Roland Barthes termed the 'that which has been' of photographic reference); instead, it translates the visual into easily manipulable digital code. And with its severing from reality, the image is cast into the realm of imagination.

Developments in digital technology have paralleled, not surprisingly, a gradual demotion of photography's documentary tendencies in practice. According to the Canadian photographer Jeff Wall, whose work bears precedence for Tabrizian's own, the aim of art photography has become a matter of creating 'pictures', for which the verification of truth is no longer at issue. Rather, what counts is the image's expressive power which, by mixing the conventions of narrative painting and computer imaging, it might deliver in any number of creative ways. Of course, Tabrizian's practice has been dedicated to making certain kinds of pictures, imaging in particular the ennui of our contemporary existence under advanced global capitalism, which Stuart Hall, in an insightful essay on the artist's work, termed 'a critique of the everyday life of contemporary corporate-post-modernity and its "systems" of representation.'

In this regard, Tabrizian's images of the hard, slick surfaces of cold corporate architecture, and her scenes of superficial networking ceremonies attended by non-individuals subsumed by their monotonous business-world uniforms, resonate with the classic accounts of postmodernism such as Fredric Jameson's analysis of its schizophrenic social fragmentation, waning of affect, and amnesiac fixation on the present at the expense of historical consciousness. That Tabrizian's figures appear trapped in this dystopic milieu perhaps explains their resulting existential crises – the episodes of sudden catatonic immobility, aimless wandering, regressive withdrawal, even suicide – which appear as the dysfunctional environment's damaging consequences on human life.

Of course, with almost everyone now familiar with the tricks of digital photography, it is impossible to view Tabrizian's work as pursuing the same postmodernist strategy of critical mimicry as practiced decades ago – consider Robert Longo's drawings of businessmen caught in moments of paroxysm, or Cindy Sherman's ersatz citations of classic Hollywood cinema, their critical power deriving from the exposure of the artifice of representation. These earlier models parody what they repeat, but with a telling excess or difference, also signalling that the critique is motivated by a desire to resist identifying with those enticing movie images. For Tabrizian's part, the obviously staged quality of her images – which reference the art of quotation that first emerged roughly thirty years ago – brings into view the typical emotional indifference with which social breakdown is currently encountered in the mass media and movie industry. Exemplary in this regard is her series *The Perfect Crime* (2003), its intimation of shady corporate dealings recalling the films of Quentin Tarantino in which violence becomes leisurely entertainment. Yet the melancholy aspect of Tabrizian's photographs owes to the fact that they anticipate the blasé viewer who is also no longer moved by the critical exposure of the social indifference towards others. By identifying that apathy, they seek to transform it.

Tabrizian's photographs are poignant because she links current-day social isolation and psychological breakdown not only to the economic alienation of corporate-post-modernity, but also to various representational factors, including digital technology, the eclipse of the real in post-documentary photography (and film) and the reign of postmodern simulation. So what of *Tehran 2006* and *Border*, which depict real people, rather than nameless characters set in fictional scenarios, even if those fictions bear a certain social truth? Despite *Border*'s return to reality, accompanied by the personal testimonies of its subjects, the series' dramatic titles and fragmented positions, awkward pauses and unexplained behaviour – like so many film stills taken out of context – maintain the photographic uncertainty that has long guided Tabrizian's work. In other words, the expression of the impossibility of feeling at home abroad as much as in one's place of origin (as is clear in *Tehran*'s depiction of socially

isolated figures situated under the domineering portraits of Iran's rulers) means that the return to photographic reality cannot offer the security that might salve the existential anxiety accompanying migration.

While the experience of loneliness would seem to inspire the longing for empathy, caring relationships and comforting images of home, Tabrizian refrains from offering such nostalgic fixes. Instead we face figures who stare into the distance, their suggested imaginings ultimately unavailable to us. In this vein, her photographs show that documentary's representation of the fullness of subjective reality is ultimately never possible, for there is always something more to people than mere images of them can capture. Like the longing figures in *Border*, our only recourse is to invent that meaning for ourselves, and hopefully escape our indifference.

Mitra Tabrizian in Conversation with Rose Issa

RI: This exhibition at Tate Britain shows a selection of your recent works. They reveal an important shift from your earlier photographs, which were fictional and staged, using professional models and actors, not unlike film posters. Your recent work is more documentary in style, with real people re-enacting their own stories. Does it reflect the influence of Iranian cinema, which in the late 1980s and early 1990s introduced a genre that I call 'real fictions'? The Iranian cinematic language champions the poetics of everyday life in a new style, blurring the boundaries between fiction and reality, feature and documentary.

MT: The earlier work focuses on corporate culture and is deliberately 'constructed', cold and flat, although I didn't always use professional actors, or produce staged images, so there hasn't been such a clear-cut shift. *Silent Majority* (2001), for instance, is in effect a 'documentary' piece – if what we mean by documentary is the use of real locations, real people, undirected and spontaneous. In *Lost Time* (2002), I mixed actors and non-actors, some recreating their own experiences.

For the recent work on Iran I wanted to deviate from the usual representations in photography and video: the social documentary or journalistic approach, or constructed images, often on a 'big' subject, or the tendency to exoticise. Rather, the work, as you mentioned, echoes contemporary Iranian cinema, often using non-actors and focusing on an apparently 'small' subject, treated allegorically to allude to wider social issues.

RI: Let us talk about *Tehran 2006* (2006) – a key moment of reflection on Iran. Most of your earlier work focused on issues concerning the West. Despite using ordinary people, and having a 'documentary' look, *Tehran 2006* is still a very highly conceived and structured panorama. Can you speak about the concept behind the work and how you realised the final image?

MT: *Tehran 2006* looks at the reality of everyday life and the ordinary in extraordinary times.

Tehran is a modern city like any other, overpopulated and heavily congested. But I chose this particular spot, a newly built post-revolution landscape still in development which, despite the cityscape in the background and new buildings in the foreground, looks as if it's in the middle of nowhere, with people that have nowhere to go. All the characters 'play' themselves. The crowd is a mixture of people who are struggling: a taxi driver, factory worker, builder, cleaner, dressmaker, servant or caretaker. It will be these people, already living on the edge, who are hit most if the economic sanctions continue, or in the event of military action. At another level, and in the context of the current 'dispute' in which Iran is seen as a threat or a victim, to focus on ordinary life and the everyday could suggest both that Iranians are not necessarily a threat (as certain countries fear) and that they cannot easily be intimidated by external pressure (as the Americans, in particular, tend to think), and life goes on and people survive. These views are strongly shared by the majority in Iran today. So, conceptually the project is concerned with 'survival'.

RI: The *Border* series (2005–6), about the East in the West, is of Iranians in exile in the UK, resiliently waiting. What made you want to make this series? Was it a sense of displacement and a certain desire to return?

MT: *Border* concentrates on the fantasy of return, no matter how slight, only to demonstrate the underlying reality, as Stuart Hall observes, that 'migration is a one way trip'. Having interviewed the volunteers who participated in this project, what emerged, despite their diverse case histories, is that in the realm of fantasy, they all feel as if they have 'unfinished business' and therefore are waiting. So in this project each narrative implies the notion of 'waiting', used as a metaphor to indicate both the bleakness of the situation – things may never change, certainly not in the near future – and a more complex reading of not having any 'home' to return to, even if things will eventually change: the fantasy of 'home' is always very different from the reality of what you may encounter when you get there. In short, the concept of waiting is portrayed more like Beckett's *Waiting for Godot* – rather than a realist interpretation. As Salman Rushdie noted, 'exile is a dream of glorious return that must remain unrealized'.

Shot in London, *Border* portrays individuals on their own in an unfamiliar environment; there is a sense of displacement and solitude, creating a *mise-en-scene* which is unsettling. *Tehran 2006* portrays a crowd in a familiar environment, yet the image still connotes a sense of seclusion stressing the alienation felt by Iranians today. What links the two projects is hardship and isolation on both sides of the 'border', dismantling the fantasy Iranians may have of both the West or the East. Those who live in Iran tend to idealise life in the West and those who live outside long for 'home'. But what both groups have in common is the will to survive – evident in the stories of the participants in these two projects – and an enormous resilience. To survive is ultimately to have the capacity to negotiate new positions, which means the necessary redefinition of the past and present. To survive is also not to give up, and (in one definition) not to give in to whatever ordeal one is facing; it is, in a less orthodox way, as Homi Bhabha states, to 'resist'. And thus survival becomes a strategy of resistance.

RI: I think most people from the Middle East have no other choice than to develop a spirit of resistance, whether living in the East or the West. We are in a way between a rock and a hard place. We have to carve a perilous path to find a way to save our mental space. We have to resist misrepresentation or non-representation of our intellectuals, artists and even ordinary members of the public. We have to fight censorship, false promises and archaic laws that exist not to protect the public but to silence it, in East and in West. We have to find the loopholes – something that Iranian film-makers and artists have mastered. In your *Border* series I see more resilience than resistance, a sense of unease, the general dissatisfaction of people who are neither happy in the West nor in the East. I think that the future is better perceived by those on 'the cultural edge of intersecting worlds', as the philosopher

Dariush Shayegan labels the 'migrants' that we are, living tirelessly in border zones.

Let us move to the West, and your work since 2000 on corporate culture. *Silent Majority* has almost an opposite look to *Tehran 2006*. Is it about altogether another class of people, another setting at the heart of London's finance centre, Canary Wharf, with colder colours, a crowd rather than individuals, a still photograph that represents a corporate pulse?

MT: I was inspired by the work of French sociologist-philosopher Jean Baudrillard, in particular his analysis of contemporary culture, which is illuminating as it provides an insight into a new condition and social experience that we are all facing, including what we may call 'social depression'. At a literal level, *Silent Majority* is concerned with depression, or more accurately the invisibility of it in today's society of indifference. In a corporate world where one has to compete at any cost, succeed at any cost, depression has become the norm. At a more philosophical level, the work attempts to evoke Baudrillard's world of simulation, a fractal culture where 'the people' are compelled into silence, into an extremity of indifference and conformity.

RI: I am not a philosopher, and yet I can see clearly that modernity is in crisis with its focus on celebrity culture, and money as the ultimate sign of success. Which brings us back to your take on corporate culture in *Beyond the Limits* and *Lost Time*.

MT: Set in the future, *Beyond the Limits* (2000–1) constructs fragments of everyday life, each portraying an event in which something has gone 'wrong'. Again I was interested in Baudrillard's notion of 'implosion', the point where things turn in upon themselves and produce the opposite effects to those intended. I was looking at what is happening now and pushing it one step further. For instance, in the image of the crowd networking, what's gone wrong is the disappearance of art. Or, a man falling. Is it suicide or murder? Or, within the all-powerful global technostructure, the distinction between the two has now become blurred. A metaphorical murder then; having to function within the world of uncertainty, where the logic is maximising profit at any cost, and concepts such as 'over-worked', 'security' or 'future' have no meaning.

Lost Time continues the critique of corporate culture. It portrays business men and women in their forties and fifties, dressed for work in working hours yet appearing in 'non-work' places. Some refuse to leave the house, others are 'lost' in the city.

More than ever the young are fetishised and the not so young are unwanted. They are increasingly encouraged to take early retirement. Look at the current restructuring plans happening in various institutions. And this project was made in 2002. One of the participants, a BBC producer, was asked to re-apply for his own job on a series he had created himself!

So the work addresses the concept of ageism by portraying the individual's sense of premature inactivity, unwantedness and ultimately 'failure' in a society where work and competition seem to overpower all other values. On another level, the work is an ironic commentary on the ethos of the present time; once we are stripped of our corporate identity, what's left to hang on to?

RI: This is an important observation. Galleries keep asking me who the young, up-and-coming talents are, without ever knowing anything about the previous generation. I would like them to ask who the most relevant and interesting artists are rather than the newest, or what the best as yet unknown works are. So there is certainly an obsession with youth in the contemporary art world.

What about *The Perfect Crime*?

MT: *The Perfect Crime* (2003) focuses on violence and people's indifference. In a society over-saturated with violence, where we've become immune to it, the title 'The Perfect Crime' is used ironically to refer less to the crime than to people's reaction: crime becomes perfect when no one cares. Reminiscent of stills from crime movies, the work brings together an aesthetic device favoured by Henri Cartier-Bresson (the camera focusing on people's reaction rather than the event itself) with the conceptual approach of Japanese film director Takeshi Kitano, whose movies intentionally accentuate violence to critique its fetishisation in contemporary cinema.

RI: And the *Wall House* series?

MT: *Wall House #2* (2007) was a commissioned project on the work of the American architect John Hejduk, a solitary, enigmatic character, a 'misfit' who was known for his lyrical and conceptual projects, and who didn't particularly care

if his designs were realised. As he said in an interview, 'it is misguided to think your working drawing must always end up as a cut-and-dried building.' Only two of his projects were ever built. Wall House #2 was initially designed in 1973 as a residential house and was built in Groningen, Holland in 2001, and is now a museum. My focus was on the idea of 'public versus private', as for the most part you can see in and through the house, with no doors inside.

Considering that Hejduk was more interested in ideas than in the practicality of realising them, the breakdown of the distinction between the private and the public in Wall House #2 could be interpreted as a revolutionary architectural design, providing a 'mutual voyeurism'. It could also be read as a critical observation and a prediction of contemporary life, where, in the world of surveillance, 'Big Brother' and reality television, the notion of the private is disappearing.

The Italian director Michelangelo Antonioni also preferred intellectual restlessness to a desire for comfort and pragmatism. Like Hejduk, he was a visionary, an outsider who deviated from the traditional approach to storytelling. It was the non-event that interested him, that 'filled' his films. Depicting the characters as empty and aimless, his films often focused on alienation in the modern world, or, as one of his more observant critics accurately notes, 'this alienation seems to be an effect of a specific social organization, rather than a general response to the difficulties of modern life … it is not life in general that is meaningless, but this particular of social life.'

The narratives in this project place Antonioni's characters in Hejduk's house, constructing two sets of images, shot inside and outside, looking in to the most private spaces in the house (toilet, bedroom, kitchen), and looking out to the exterior surrounding the house. The latter is presented in this exhibition. Here the house is used as a symbol of spectacle rather than a space for privacy and comfort.

The work uses a different aesthetic to previous ones: less sharp, less saturated, referencing faded film stills and posters. And following Antonioni's concept, the narratives attempt to depict 'interiority', that is, interior emotional states, in the form of gestures, expressions and interactions between the characters. What brings the two sets of images together is isolation. The characters are either portrayed on their own or, if they appear with others, there seems to be a lack of communication, a disconnection signifying 'aloneness', much as with Antonioni's characters, whose films ultimately set out to examine the relationship between the individuals and their environment by examining the people themselves, to see, as he asked, 'what remained inside the individual' in a post-war society. Similarly, we may speculate, what will remain of individuals today in a life lacking in purpose, in a world with no privacy, no secrecy, no enigma?

RI: Would you say that alienation and a sort of physical and mental no man's land form the common ground of most of your recent work?

MT: More accurately what we may call the crisis of contemporary culture both in the West and the East seems to be the recurrent theme.

RI: As an Iranian who came to London, do you feel on the periphery or part of the English art scene? And in light of current debates, would you consider yourself as an Iranian artist, or an artist?

MT: I never felt part of the British art scene. My work was mainly shown outside the UK. There seems to be more interest abroad than here.

The question as to whether to position oneself as an 'Iranian artist' or an 'artist' is a difficult one, as both are open to misinterpretations; the first could be read as reductionist and the second as apolitical. I prefer the term 'cultural practitioner' with a special interest in, or concern for, Iran.

February 2008

Wall House #2 2007

with Zadoc Nava

Tehran 2006 2006

Border 2005-6

with Andy Golding and Zadoc Nava
stories compiled with Christopher Williams

The Long Wait

Deadly Affair

Arash, once a soldier in the Shah's Imperial army who makes a living as a mechanic. After the fall of the Shah, there were several attempts on his life, and he had to leave. He speaks old Farsi, wears a bullet-proof jacket and sees himself as 'a warrior prepared to die for the cause.' Passionate about the Iran he once knew, he 'will go on waiting until it's a free country again.' A man with no country and no family, his estranged wife does not allow him to see his only son, but his dedicated cat follows him everywhere.

Man with a Past

Rasool, a private and proud man who 'has seen a lot', and does not like to talk about the past. He works as a taxi driver. What forced him to leave was a hard life. But he's still ambivalent about Iran: 'When I was there I wanted to be here, and now that I'm here I want to be there.' It's a solitary life. 'Driving a taxi at night is well paid, but dangerous – especially if you don't speak the language.' Back in Iran, when the pressure built up, he used to take off. 'Driving through a deserted landscape can be very calming; it clears the mind. You can see decision in apparent indecision. The trouble is, you're always expecting something to happen. And nothing ever does.'

27

Lost Steps

Parvaneh, an actress and writer. She works as an advisor to refugees, but prefers not to talk about her past. Admires the British theatre which has taught her a lot – and has written and acted in several plays, mainly about women. 'There are stories to tell, but then a price to pay.' She came to England by chance: 'It could have been anywhere, we just had to leave.' And although she's been here for years, and has enjoyed and benefited from the cultural opportunities, she has never felt settled. 'I can't get used to the weather. I thrive on sun, but can't find it here. It's shining in Iran – but I don't recognise the place!'

Road to Nowhere

Mahmood, an ex-engineer who sells carpets. As a young man, he fought for years against the Shah and had to leave. After the revolution, he returned, but was forced to leave again: 'Things did not work out!' He came to England with just twenty pounds in his pocket and worked in a bakery, a restaurant and as a tourist guide. He never saw his parents again. He'd been close to them. Both died not long ago. As for the rest of the family, 'it's been a long time. The ones I knew are dead, and the ones who remain I don't know.' He is tired of travelling, selling, a 'nomadic life' and loneliness. What he misses most is Iranian mountains. One day, he'd like to show his sons his home town in the south, well aware that the town won't be the same: 'Poverty changes people; friends become enemies.' An outsider here and an outcast there, one thing he knows at least – he does not want to die in this country.

The Perfect Crime 2003

with Andy Golding and Zadoc Nava

White Nights

Private Enemy

On Dangerous Ground

Lost Time 2002

Oxford & Cherwell Valley College
Learning Resources

Silent Majority 2001

List of Works

p. 17
From the series *Wall House #2* 2007
C-type print
122 × 159 cm
Courtesy the artist

p. 18
From the series *Wall House #2* 2007
C-type print
122 × 153 cm
Courtesy the artist

p. 19
From the series *Wall House #2* 2007
C-type print
122 × 153 cm
Courtesy the artist

p. 20
From the series *Wall House #2* 2007
C-type print
122 × 153 cm
Courtesy the artist

pp. 22–3
Tehran 2006 2006
C-type light jet print
101 × 302 cm
Victoria and Albert Museum

p. 25
The Long Wait
From the series *Border* 2005–6
C-type print
122 × 153 cm
Courtesy the artist

p. 26
Deadly Affair
From the series *Border* 2005–6
C-type print
122 × 153 cm
Private Collection, Zurich

p. 27
Man with a Past
From the series *Border* 2005–6
C-type print
122 × 153 cm
Courtesy the artist

p. 28
Lost Steps
From the series *Border* 2005–6
C-type print
122 × 153 cm
Courtesy the artist

p. 29
Road to Nowhere
From the series *Border* 2005–6
C-type print
122 × 153 cm
Courtesy the artist

p. 31
White Nights
From the series
The Perfect Crime 2003
C-type print
122 × 153 cm
Courtesy the artist

p. 32
Private Enemy
From the series
The Perfect Crime 2003
C-type print
122 × 153 cm
Courtesy the artist

p. 33
On Dangerous Ground
From the series
The Perfect Crime 2003
C-type print
122 × 153 cm
Courtesy the artist

p. 35
From the series *Lost Time* 2002
C-type print
122 × 154 cm
Courtesy the artist

p. 36
From the series *Lost Time* 2002
C-type print
122 × 145 cm
Courtesy the artist

p. 37
From the series *Lost Time* 2002
C-type print
122 × 157 cm
Courtesy the artist

pp. 38–9
Silent Majority 2001
C-type light jet print
122 × 214 cm
Courtesy the artist

p. 41
From the series
Beyond the Limits 2000–1
C-type print
122 × 162 cm
Courtesy the artist

p. 42
From the series
Beyond the Limits 2000–1
C-type print
124 × 177 cm
Courtesy the artist

Select Biography

Born in Iran. Lives and works in London. Currently teaches at the University of Westminster.

Solo Exhibitions

2008
Galerie Caprice Horn, Berlin.

2006
Moderna Musset, Stockholm.
BBK, Bilbao.
Künstlerhaus Bethanien, Berlin.
Museum Folkwang, Essen, Germany.

1998
Minimal Utopia, Camera Austria Gallery, Graz, Austria.

1994
Hippolyte Gallery, Helsinki.
Galleri Index, Centre of Photography, Stockholm.

1988
Cornerhouse, Manchester.

1987
National Museum of Photography, Film and Television, Bradford.

1986
Galerie Château d'Eau, Toulouse.

1985
Screen Memories, Perspectief, Rotterdam.
Gallery 400, Chicago (touring).
Stills Gallery, Edinburgh.

Selected Group Exhibitions

2008
Street and Studio: An Urban History of Photography, Tate Modern, London.

2007
C International Photo, Phillips de Pury, New York.
Wall House Project, Noorderlicht Gallery, Groningen, Holland.
FotoArtFestival, Bielsko-Biala, Poland.

2006
Italian Pavilion, Tenth Venice Biennale of Architecture.
Voodoo Macbeth, De la Warr Pavilion in association with Brighton Photo Biennial.

2005
Safe: An Exhibition of Contemporary Art, Karlskrona Art Gallery and Blekinge Museum, Karlskrona, Sweden.

2004
Far Near Distance: New Positions of Contemporary Iranian Artists, Haus der Kulturen der Welt, Berlin.
Lumo '04 Triennial of Contemporary Photography, Jyväskylä Art Museum, Finland.

2003
Aletheia: The Real of Concealment, Göteborgs Konstmuseum, Gothenburg, Sweden.
Veil, Museum of Modern Art, Oxford (touring).

2001
Inhabiting, Gallery Lelong, New York.

1999
London: Post-Colonial City, Architectural Association, London.

1996
Gender: Beyond Memory, Tokyo Metropolitan Museum of Photography, Tokyo.
Family, Nation, Tribe, Community Shift, Haus der Kulturen der Welt, Berlin.

1995
The Outburst of Signs: Art at the Interfaces of Gender and Race, Künstlerwerkstatt Lothringerstrasse, Munich.

1994
Le Shuttle, Künstlerhaus Bethanien, Berlin.
Public Domain, Centre d'Art Santa Mònica, Barcelona.

1993
Mistaken Identities, University of California, Santa Barbara.
Museum Folkwang, Essen (touring).

1992
History Present, Museum Folkwang, Essen.
*Fine Material for a Dream …?
A Reappraisal of Orientalism: Nineteenth- and Twentieth-Century Fine Art and Popular Culture*, Harris Museum, Preston.

1991
Shocks to the System: Social and Political Issues in Recent British Art from the Arts Council Collection, Royal Festival Hall, London (touring).
Public Images, Forum Stadtpark, Graz, Austria.

1990
Contemporary Social Documentary, Fotobiennial, Art History Centre, Vigo, Spain.

1989
Mysterious Coincidences, The Photographers' Gallery, London (touring).
Shifting Focus, Serpentine Gallery, London (touring).
Through the Looking Glass: Photographic Art in Britain 1945–1989, Barbican Art Gallery, London.
The Boundaries of Photography, Alvar Aalto Museum, Jyväskylä, Finland.
Some Notions on Marginality, Grey Art Gallery, New York University, New York.

1988
The Other Body, Photographic
Resource Centre, Boston University,
Boston.
International Photography, Metronom,
Barcelona.
Reflections on the Media, Perspectief,
Rotterdam.
*Towards the Photograph as a Vulgar
Document*, Optica Gallery, Montreal.
*Sexual Difference: Both Sides of the
Camera*, Wallach Art Gallery,
Columbia University, New York.

1987
The Body Politic, The Photographers'
Gallery, London.

1986
International Photography, Arles
International Gallery, Arles.

1985
Magnificent Obsession, ARC Gallery,
Toronto.
Impostors, Interim Art, London.
Towards a Bigger Picture, Victoria
and Albert Museum, London.
European Women Photographers Today,
Torino Fotografia, Torino, Italy.
Beyond the Purloined Image, Riverside
Studios, London.
*The Way We Live Now: Beyond Social
Documentary*, P.S.1, New York.
Phototextes, Les Musée d'Art et
d'Histoire, Geneva.
Five Photographers, Institute of
Contemporary Arts, London.
The Actress, The Photographers'
Gallery, London.

Films

2004
Co-writer and Director of
The Predator, AHRB Innovation
Awards (Arts and Humanities
Research Board), 35 mm, 28 minutes.

1993
Writer and Director of *Journey of
No Return*, British Film Institute,
16 mm, 23 minutes.

1990
Writer and Director of *The Third
Woman*, British Film Institute,
16 mm, 20 minutes.

Publications

2004
Beyond the Limits (with an
introduction by Stuart Hall), Steidl,
Göttingen, Germany.

1990
Correct Distance (with an introduction
by Griselda Pollock), Cornerhouse,
Manchester.

Public Collections

Alvar Aalto Museum, Jyväskylä,
Finland
Arts Council of Great Britain
Institute of Contemporary Art,
Boston
Moderna Musset, Stockholm
Museum Folkwang, Essen, Germany
Tokyo Metropolitan Museum of
Photography, Tokyo
National Museum of Photography,
Film and Television, Bradford
Sparkasse Essen, Germany
Stichting Fotografie Noorderlicht,
Groninger, Netherlands
Victoria and Albert Museum,
London
Waikato Museum of Art and
History, Hamilton, New Zealand

Retouching: Dennis Tuffnell,
Core Digital

The artist would like to thank:
Zadoc Nava; Andy Golding,
University of Westminster; Alastair
Thompson, Core Digital; Michael
Dyer Associates and Roy Bass;
Mario Capaldi, Bob Martin and
Karin Askham; David Freeman,
University of Westminster;
the MA students at University
of Westminster who assisted with
the project; and all the participants
in the photographs.

Border funded by Arts Council
England and the Arts and
Humanities Research Council.

Wall House #2 funded by
Noorderlicht, Netherlands.

Tehran 2006 funded by Arts Council
England and the Arts and
Humanities Research Council.
Lighting: Dariush Kiani, Fanoos
Photo, Iran. Special thanks to:
Siamac Akhavan; Hamid Severi at
the Museum of Contemporary Art,
Tehran; Shadi Ghadirian; and all
the participants in the photographs.
The project is dedicated to the
memory of Mrs Mohamadi, one
of the participants.